TEMPTATION BY WATER

Also by Diane Lockward

What Feeds Us
Eve's Red Dress
Against Perfection (chapbook)

Temptation by Water

Diane Lockward

To Mau...
Happy ... unite at
Girl Talk.

Diane Lockward

WIND PUBLICATIONS
2010

International Standard Book Number 978-1-936138-12-8
Library of Congress Catalog Number 2010927962

First edition

Cover art by Brian Rumbolo
Author photo by Lloyd Grover

Acknowledgments

Grateful acknowledgment is made to the following journals in which some of the poems in this collection first appeared:

Caesura: "'No soup for you!'"

Cold Mountain Review: "'Your dreams miss you'"

Contemporary American Voices: "Kerfuffle," "Twilight"

Crab Creek Review: "Side Effects"

Edison Literary Review: "When Pigs Flee"

Georgetown Review: "There Where Love Had Been"

Harvard Review: "Seventh-Grade Science Project"

Ibbetson Street Review: "Capturing the Image"

Innisfree Poetry Journal: "For One Who Crumbles in Spring," "Pleasure," "Spying on My New Neighbors"

Inside Jersey: "A Murmuration of Starlings," "Stripping the Lemon"

Lips: "Filbert," "How Sarah Wins the Essay Contest"

The Medulla Review: "Phone in a White Room"

Melusine, or Woman in the 21st Century: "Bathing in *Forest Dusk*," "Implosion," "What He Doesn't Know"

Mezzo Cammin: "Onion," "The Very Smell of Him"

Naugatuck River Review: "My Mother Turns Her Back"

New York Quarterly: "Flash," "It Runs This Deep"

Pank: "Happy Hour," "My Dark Lord," "Why I Won't Have a Full-Body Massage"

Poet Lore: "A Knock at the Door," "Leaving in Pieces," "To a Potato"

The Raintown Review: "The Jesus Potato"

Rattle: "Love Song with Plum"

Red-Headed Stepchild: "*Prunis Persica*"

Slab: "Nostrum"

Spoon River Poetry Review: "Weather Report," "Without Words for It"

Studio: "Supplication to Water"

Sweet: A Literary Confection: "Learning to Live Alone"

Talking River Review: "The Desolation of Wood," "If Only Humpty Dumpty Had Been a Cookie"

Tiferet: "Birdhouse"

Valparaiso Poetry Review: "April at the Arboretum," "'How Is a Shell Like Regret?,'" "Hunger in the Garden," "Temptation by Water," "The Temptation of Mirage"

Web del Sol: "Ecdysiast," "Woman with Fruit"

"'How Is a Shell Like Regret?'" was reprinted in the *Alhambra Poetry Calendar 2010*, edited by Shafiq Naz (Alhambra Press).

"'How Is a Shell Like Regret?'" was reprinted in the textbook, *The Working Poet: 75 Exercises and a Poetry Anthology* (Autumn House Press, 2009).

"A Murmuration of Starlings" was reprinted in *Pirene's Fountain.*

"Seventh-Grade Science Project" appeared on *Poetry Daily* on August 1, 2008.

"Temptation by Water" was reprinted in the 2010 issue of *Manorborn.*

For my uncle
George L. Striebing
1924-2009
dulcia somnia

Contents

Four

Five

. . . our real desire is to be tempted enough.

—Augustus William Hare

Temptation by Water

—after *The Open Window*, by Henri Matisse

Beyond the frame, a woman stands before
the open window—two shutters pulled inside
frame the sea beyond, so three-dimensional
she could wade into it and board a blue-hulled
boat, ride the waves of color—vermillion, jade,
gold, a slash of violet—could tread the razzle
of light on water, and here and there a splash
of black, like shadows foreboding something
she cannot name.

      She floats inside the frame,
like Alice free-falling down the hole, enters this
other world, leaves her work on the windowsill,
her terracotta pots of red blossoms, drifts towards
the simulation of clouds, turquoise horizon, the sea
like liquid emeralds, a kind of paradise, not one
human in sight, not one person she can name.

One

Weather Report

It's one of those nights when sleep
is elusive and the TV runs non-stop,
so I'm still half-awake
when the weatherman says,
"Devastation results from *desire*."

He hesitates, as if startled, then corrects,
"No, I mean *disaster,* the devastation
that comes from earthquakes, wind,
fire, and flood," but I'm already
in complete agreement and thinking
about a man who does push-ups
not to lift himself off the ground
but to hold down the earth
and how the earth sometimes cracks
and it has nothing to do with weather,
and I remember storm chasers
who drive hundreds of miles
to be right on the spot when the tornado hits
to see the eye of the storm
while others carry that eye inside,
and once more I see that woman
who stood in a burning building
and dropped her child out the window
believing someone would catch him
and that other woman who prays
for the hands to pull her boy
from the flames of his addictions,

and I think of the model who for eight hours
clung to a tree while the tidal wave broke
her beautiful body and swept her lover away.

All night I think about metaphors,
how one thing is always like some other thing,
the weather outside and the weather inside,
how a slip of the tongue can change
desire into disaster, how desire and water
can sweep us away, and how we are all
looking for someone to push back
the waves, to grab hold of us, and keep us
here, pressed to this earth.

Implosion

Today an abandoned power plant in Tampa.
Beautiful, really, the way the building fell in
on itself, enveloped in a plume of smoke,
bricks tumbling like disaster in slow motion.

Convergence of math and physics,
this fine art of blasting.

Not one person hurt by flying debris,
epitomic destruction of what's not needed—

like the small building of the heart,
its pumping machine grown idle,
furnace snuffed, the years of vacancy.
Grief, a vagrant huddled in the corridor.
Brick edifice fragile as shells.

Comes the condemnation, the inrush of air,
the structural blowdown.

This is the way a heart melts.
No fire, no flames, no heat.
Just the soft mushroom of dust and ash,
the quiet collapse inside.

Leaving in Pieces

One morning I awoke
and found myself married
to a bald man.
This was unexpected and unpleasant.
I'd married my husband for his hair.
My mother always said
it was lustrous, and she was right.
My husband had lustrous hair.

Not so hard to take when black
turned to silver, but when something
turned to nothing!
And there on the pillow
a fully exposed skull,
forcing me to contemplate
weighty subjects I preferred to ignore,
like my own mortality.

The hairless head was yellowish-white
and shiny as a peeled clove of garlic.
I saw its imperfections—
wens and protrusions, moles and warts,
pimples and wedges of bone.

Outside our window grackles twittered,
shook their lustrous feathers,
and mocked my loss.
For consolation, I bought a dog,

a black Labrador retriever.
His thick fur reminded me
of my husband's missing hair.

I taught my new dog to heel and obey.
I taught him to fetch.
He brought back sticks and tennis balls,
but not my husband's lustrous hair.

I moved him into the big house
and my husband into the doghouse.
It seemed a fair exchange.
The dog at least did not complain.

He worked his way into my bed.
His liquid eyes, his lustrous fur,
I found irresistible.
We frolicked and then we slept,
undisturbed by nightmares or regrets.

We hardly minded the howls
of our poor bald dog as he absorbed
the lesson of loss
and made mournful noise
throughout the night.

What He Doesn't Know

This is the season of the centipede.
Concealed by night, he crawls
across the ceiling,
here to terrify but not to harm.

How easily he travels at breakneck speed,
up the drains and down the walls.
Each of his one hundred legs securely clings,
each foot so soft and light he sounds no alarm.

On his head he bears a pair of jointed
feelers and two sets of jaws.
His body's many-segmented and long,
yet among the excess of legs, not one arm.

The foremost pair of legs behind his head—
two poison claws,
once legs, then evolved to fangs,
though he's oblivious to the bite of Time.

He has no philosophy, obeys no creed,
needs only pipes in which he trawls
undetected, moved by metal's ping
and an instinctual compulsion to roam.

When hunger compels him to feed,
he extends his predacious mandibles
and silently captures his victim, swiftly killing
with a lethal injection of venom.

This creature breeds
without reason or romance, no heart calls,
no courtship dance, just sex without feeling,
no need to love, no desire stoked to flame.

Lucky little arthropod,
without our human flaws.
He has no poetry, no art, no songs,
but knows no fear when darkness enters a room.

Pleasure

No golden fleece, apple, parachute, or purse,
but that sexy red dress you couldn't afford now on sale,
Cape Cod light captured on the artist's easel,
a bowl of mushroom barley soup to slurp,
and under the sofa the pearl
you thought you'd lost, a rule
broken without penalty, no need to reap
the wild oats you sowed. Each night you ease
into dreams, and while you sleep,
the skin cream you bought really does erase
lines and wrinkles. Outside, goldfinches bright as lemon peels.

Stripping the Lemon

—after *Strip-Tease,* by Jeff Hayes

I could be peeled
 like that, in liberal
  strips, one end
   to the other, skin
    lifted off in a spiral,
     your hands aswirl,
      knife slicing, flesh
       entire, membrane
       intact, white
       like a bridal veil,
      an immaculate
     undergarment,
    fingers stroking
   top end and bottom,
  tips scented
with zest, stroke
of the blade
missing a patch
 at the top, tip
  a generous nipple.
   I could be
    your enigma,
    your oblong
     of confusion,
      spherical paradox.
      Would you lift
      off this skin,

13

let it float
like a boa?
Would you grate
my goldfinch
gold, my sparkling
sun, my outrageous
egg yolk yellow?
Would you take me
as I am, or squeeze
and squeeze, make me
what I would not be—
a sorbet, a pudding, a pie?

Why I Won't Have a Full-Body Massage

This doughy flesh
does not want a stranger's fingers
kneading it.

This body turns its back on the squeeze,
stroke, and thump of therapeutic hands,
pods of fingers at vital points, pressure points,
points at which I might capitulate.

Each pore of my hyperkeratotic husk closes
to creams and balms, the ooze and glide
of lotions and gels.

This sorry sack of skin refuses
a stranger's gaze, my naked, dimpled sins
exposed, declines the lure of improved circulation,
chakras cleared and balanced in perfect polarity,
the rush of nutrients through muscles aching
for touch, won't allow fingertips to prod
the soft surface zones.

Every dermal cell says *No* to aromatherapy oils—
peach and mango, scent of sea breeze—
says *No* to the slow slide of warm stones
over hills and valleys of flesh, the rock
and roll of knuckles and palms,
hot packs strategically placed along the flint
of spine,

on fire again, all sparks and flames,
each muscle burning and rising
towards the familiarity of tender hands
kneading it.

My Mother Turns Her Back

The snake on my mother's
     back thickens, a python
          bulging with rats. Knotted

          and gnarled, it switches
     her. She bends, she bows,
she tips her hat. She twists

into a question mark, her
     body confused by the
          puzzle of vertebrae,

          its pieces scattered
     like an errant jigsaw.
Something inside me

constricts as words with
     spurs slip into the spaces
          between us—*stenosis,*

          osteoporosis, cervical
spondylosis. The rogue
bone multiplies, proliferates,

spreads like fungus across
     the diseased bark of her
          back, spine multi-fisted,

            each fist clenched and
        knuckled, each delivering
a blow. I watch my mother

grow down, as if she carries
        a burden of basket, as if
                already greeting the earth.

Hunger in the Garden

Dead things litter the grass—branches,
leaves, needles—last summer's detritus.

Four deer nibble my rhododendron, consuming
spring's promised blossoms.

Unflowered now, no burst of red and pink this year,
no sweetness of laurel.

Azaleas, too, surrender to teeth, to hunger's
chomp and winter's bite.

Winter consumes what I love and leaves
behind the wreckage of absence—

an inexplicable ache inside,
an unappeasable hunger.

Last summer a family of raccoons
emerged from the evergreens—

the father waddling in front,
mother behind with their child, his leg bleeding.

They ate seeds fallen from a feeder,
drank from the birdbath, stepped in and bathed.

Their fur sleek as seals',
the mother nuzzled her child and licked his leg.

Days later the large one came alone.
I remembered the wounded child

and imagined the mother in a bed
of leaves, unable to move.

I want to believe in regeneration, that what's
gone can return.

But only the deer come back, brazen and unafraid
when I rap the pane.

They stare at me, their eyes wide,
bodies poised, then strip away what is mine.

I want buds back on the branches,
you here in spring, your hunger and mine appeased.

Two

April at the Arboretum

Hope is the thing with feathers.
                    —Emily Dickinson

In a glass-encased room I thought of you,
far away, in the city you've flown to.
All winter I'd prayed hard for a miracle.
Now rain and ice pelted the windows,
drenched the gardens I'd wanted
to stroll. Yellow daffodils tilted,
tulips and crocus collapsed, leaves
of magnolias hung heavy with slush.

Out of purple rhododendron the first
goldfinch appeared, from forsythia, another
and another, at least a dozen, swooping
and gliding from thistle seed feeder
to tree to bush. A flock of goldfinches—
tarnished, soft, and brilliant, flying fragments
of gold, as if the sun had shattered.

Leaves of gold floated past panes of glass,
each bird without cares except to feed and fly.
All around me I heard sleet rat-a-tat-tatting,
and still the birds continued their air show.
They did not suffer from ice, but flew
in perfect formation, a miniature
roller coaster, gliding in freefall,
looping and soaring, cradled by air.

Then the rain stopped pounding, and
in that airless silence no flutter of wings, no
twitter of birdsong. I only saw those small
trapeze artists on wings, flying cordless,
without cables or net, oblivious to danger,
and I thought of you, miles away,
trembling in the cold, cold rain.

Without Words for It

She had expected something
cataclysmic when he left,
an eclipse of earth and sun,
or storm, wind, and hail,
not that there would be such silence,
not that she would be bereft of speech,
as if words, too, had abandoned her.

Without the noun of his name, no need
for adjectives to perk things up, less for adverbs.
She told herself verbs give life to sentences.
But the verbs had already betrayed her.
They shifted quickly after his absence,
switched to past tense, to the way life used to be.

The present participles disappeared,
no more call for them, though much for past, as in
the way he'd touched her or how
he'd looked at her or how she'd loved him.
Infinitives remained behind,
still valued for the way they carried on, as in
to get out of bed.

Of the conjunctions, *and* departed,
but lingered. No need to say,
You and I, much to say, *But he left.*
Only the little words remained entirely faithful,

repeating over and over again,
No, he won't come back, no, not ever.

All the sentences were simple and declarative:
He was gone.

Nostrum

Here's the medicine man who can cure most
anything. Don't call him witch doctor. He's not
a quack, no dispenser of mumbo-jumbo or clever ruse.
Whatever you have that's gone wrong, gone sour—
stomach, breath, appetite—he'll fix with moonshine rum,
elixir in a bottle. He can strum
a banjo, dance like Bojangles, conjure a storm.
Turn to him to forget what you mourn—
the house you lost, the man you loved, the child torn
in pieces. Add it up, calculate the sum
of your grief. Drink the pulp and skin, the fermented must.

Woman with Fruit

Raisins, prunes, and apricots,
the dried fruits she hungers for,
done now with ripeness, the mess of juice.

Especially she craves figs,
their turtle-textured skin, resolute stem,
quirky resilience of the pendulous bladder,

and inside the sack, seeds that crackle like grit.

If Only Humpty Dumpty
Had Been a Cookie

Chocolate chip, lumpy but popular,
sanctimonious with tradition,

irreverent snickerdoodle,
or a beautiful cookie like oatmeal lace,
delicate and chocolate-dipped,

visitor from a foreign place, Russian teacake,
shortbread with its dusty Scottish brogue,

the crisp Parisian sweetness of a meringue,
reminder that goodness breaks,

home-baked cookies from the kitchen
if only he could find his way back,
trace the trail of air scented with vanilla,
almond extract, and coconut,

the buttery goodness of his childhood
pulverized like crumbs on the floor,

a blizzard of cookies in December,
date nut bar for the lunch box,
Mississippi mud, the egalitarian black and white,

or an odd cookie, one that doesn't belong,
like a bitter espresso wafer, wimpy jelly tabby,

granola jumble with texture but no taste,
cookies that went astray,

Donna's Polish angel wings,
powdered and fragile as snowflakes,

cookies that emigrated,
crossed mountains, stowed away in ships,

slipped across borders,
and showed up in sweatshops,

flattened by the rolling pin,
cookies that staved off hunger, hid in pockets,
slept under pillows until morning light,
and did not crumble,

a blitz of cookies,
spinning through Time
like pinwheels and pfeffernuesse,

cookies earned with his yellow curls,
soft renegade cookies,
dropped, refrigerated, rolled and cut,

cookies baked by his mother,
his grandmother, a procession of women in aprons,

their slippers padding into the kitchen,
women greasing pans, pre-heating ovens,

their hands dipped in flour,
fingers kneading butter, sugar, and eggs,

women filling and enfolding him,
bringing him home, wrapped
in the unbreakable dough of their arms.

A Knock at the Door

They had come to do the repair work. As promised, they arrived between 8 AM and 7 PM. The family sat in their usual chairs. It had just begun to turn dark. Everyone was dressed casually. No one was trying to impress. The parents were slugging down cocktails. The kids were drunk on TV. Voices came from the screen. There was shouting and recriminations. Soon came the weeping, the apologies, the promises not to do it again. Everything was forgiven. The woman vaguely remem— bered loving her husband, how he had looked with the beach at his back. And then she forgot. The crew entered the room, sized up the situation, and got out the necessary tools. They turned off the TV. Repair work requires a still environment, a concentration of curative powers. They silenced the dog so he would bark no more. Fear rolled in like fog. One of them trimmed off the man's voluminous gut. Another sewed the woman's mouth shut. Dinner began to burn on the stove. The crew took a break from their work. They gobbled down beans and franks. Then they turned to the kids. The girl they dressed in a cheerleader's outfit. The boy they taught to shoot. It should have been perfect, yet they felt dissatisfied with their work. Something remained out of whack. And something inside the box hissed. They packed up their tools, shook their heads as if baffled. Some families, they had to admit, just can't be fixed.

How Sarah Wins the Essay Contest

A significant prize is at stake,
but the topic's complex: *Chaos and Order
and How They Relate to Creativity.*

She's only 12 and knows nothing of chaos,
though her father has left with the woman
her grandmother calls *that whore* and her mother
can't get out of bed for days at a time.

She has not created anything yet,
barely feels the little seeds inside,
the occasional blip blip of something
like an elevator rising and dropping,

does not know the coming chaos
of sweating, cramps, and blood, the schedule
off kilter, the skittishness of desire.

All she knows is what she's been told—be logical,
orderly, systematic, begin at the beginning,
an Introduction with Attention Grabber,
maybe a dictionary definition:

*Chaos: a condition in which chance is supreme;
inherent unpredictability; a state of utter confusion,
Order: an arrangement in sequence; a proper,
orderly, functioning condition; a state of peace,*

and next the Body, each part bolstered
with details, like flesh added to bones.
But what to say? that once the house was full
and then it wasn't? that something inside

the house had broken? that sometimes the house
was so quiet she couldn't hear anything except
the low hum of breathing?

and after she's done with the Body, a Conclusion
that pulls the parts together, extracts meaning,
and ends with a Clincher, something derived
from the soft shuffle of her mother's feet.

Learning to Live Alone

Soft as powdered sugar, snow sifted down,
its dire promise unfulfilled.
Wind rustled, and the light shifted.

A pile of bricks caught the light and shadows.
I felt an inexplicable desire
to count those bricks, to make them mine.

I had the same acquisitive urge for the birdfeeders
and sparse shrubs stripped by deer.
Something stirred inside me, like a spurt of heat.

Each of the four birdbaths suddenly seemed special,
and dozens of sweetgum balls, with their potential
for pain, strewn across the patio's reliable stones.

The rock garden where grass would not grow,
pushing up its pachysandra and yellow daylilies
that will bloom in summer.

Fallen branches, each stick and twig,
the rough bark on my pine trees—yes, *my* pine trees—
trees that capitulate to nothing,

and speckled sparrows that light on the lawn
and peck for food, heads bobbing in assent,
feathered executives reaching consensus,

then lifting in unison as if on signal,
up, up into the pines to perch on branches.
Though winter lingers, they do not abandon me.

Even the chain link fence endures, no matter what
has happened here, it grows rusty but endures.

To a Potato

I love the smell of you just before bathing,
the earth that clings to your skin,
your skin scrubbed and peeled, salted and eaten raw,
prelude to the flesh inside,

pale flesh, multitudinous pleasures,
tender and hot, steam rising from the slit,
coarse, squashy, and fluffy, requiring a ritual
of preparation, the recklessness of butter.

Bit of a bother, actually, and rather dull on your own,
always in need of enhancement.
Sliced and diced, mingled with cheddar,
sautéed, and restuffed into your skin,
the Marilyn Monroe of potatoes.

As I clutch you, plump and firm, in my palm,
I recall your humble roots, your poisonous leaves,
you among potato pickers, a crude tuber,
feeding so many mouths, sidekick to fried hunks of fish.

You are a fat, dirty spud, a misshapen blob
of starch, carbohydrates, and useless calories,
disreputable nightshade, consort to blight and famine.

Some days I think you are merely a side dish.
Nights I suffer the pangs of starvation,
tantalized by dreams of french fries,
my mouth stuffed with crisp strips of gold.

My Dark Lord

Cover me in filth, for I have lain down with pigs.
Toss me like a salad in silt and grime.

Dig a ditch and bury me up to my neck.
Pelt me with mud pies dark as fudge.

Withhold water, soap, exfoliant, and loofah.
Cleanse not my polluted flesh.

Anoint me with sediment and mineral deposits.
Make me a landfill in some desolate spot.

Abandon me to the sleazy hotel or Econo-Lodge,
for I have performed the deed of darkness.

Lay me among the potatoes.
Shroud me in a shirt of loam and peat moss.

Send an army of leeches, slugs, and maggots.
Let me be the final supper.

Baptize me anew. Christen me your own dirty girl.
Immerse my body in weeds and worms.

Break me with your shovel, backhoe, and tractor,
for I have abandoned the garden and cursed this earth.

Spying on My New Neighbors

They're tilling the soil, building a garden.
While their son's in school, they've squared
a patch of hard ground, pulled out grass and weeds,
lined up nasturtiums, snapdragons, sweet peas.

Through the scrim of evergreens, I watch them,
so close and still at first I think it's just him—
then a tangle of arms and kissing,
bodies so entwined they're almost one person or
two persons growing into each other,
twin trunks of a single tree.

Soft, smooth skin's what I'm thinking about,
how young they are, how nothing bad has happened
yet. Minutes later, they walk off the job,
his hoe dropped on top of her rake,
one whole hour before the school bell rings, before
their boy comes home, wanting Twinkies and juice.

Imagine the bulbs of their bodies planted in bed,
clothes peeled and strewn like petals, the furrowing,
the tender raking of tillable flesh, flowers blooming
from ears and eyes, the red peonies of their mouths.
Shafts of sunlight warm the garden bed.
Long tender roots shoot down, strong enough for any storm.

Three

Bathing in *Forest Dusk*

—after *Forest Dusk,* by Arlene Hyman

My fingers slide
    across your canvas,
        wiggle through the scrim
           of trees,

into the sponge
    of orange, red, and green.
        I slip through bark,
           splintered, stripped,

and bathed in the amber
    of light released.
        I forage for the gold
           at the center.

There where a heart
    has bled,
        I breathe the duff
           of deciduous leaves,

leave my sorrows
    among moss and mushrooms,
        among lilies of the valley
           and jack-in-the-pulpits.

At the base of the trees,
    a stream

of light and shadows.
Plunged into this stream,

I am cleansed.
Out of the shadows
of trees, reflections
of trees.

Out of the darkness,
light unfolds, everywhere,
topaz, ruby, emerald,
gold and more gold.

Wood nymph now, I dance
a singular dance,
my hair threaded
with leaves, body

covered with burrs,
the sweet stink
of skunk cabbage
and onion grass.

The light pulls me in,
shadows enfold me.
Your trees breathe
me in.

When Pigs Flee

*One day a little pink pig escapes from a New
Jersey farm, and in a short time it grows into
a large, aggressive and destructive feral hog.*
—*The Star-Ledger*, 8/21/08

Even piglets go stir-crazy locked up.
The little porkers want what's outside—
quail and turkey eggs,
the woodsy flavor of porcinis.

In forests and fields,
they wallow in vernal pools,
displace snakes, polliwogs, and frogs.

No longer chubby pink piglets,
no sweet-tempered peccaries or javelinas,
they are lean, mean, and hairy.

In sounders, they sneak onto golf courses
and ravage the greens, roll in the bunkers
and, with their rutting, crush the rough.

In blissful sleep, they snort and snore,
chests rising and falling in swinish dreams—
dynasty, empire, compound.

Anathema to no religion. Always in defiance
of hot dogs, pork roll, and bologna. No slab
of bacon, no scrapple, ham hocks, knockwurst,
liverwurst, cracklings, lard, or head cheese.

Never again spit-roasted in barbeque sauce.
Never again the mouth apple-stuffed.
Never again anyone's sausage.
Their unfettered feet forever unpickled.

Capturing the Image

The ocean outside my window washes me clean.
6 AM and the air's scented with seaweed and salt.
The sky turns pink, iridescent as opals.
Beach plum and sea grass sway on the sand.

No human sound, only the slap of waves,
the occasional *caw caw* of a gull.
And I who loaf in bed until 8 each day
am suddenly up with my camera.

In the Renaissance people believed that the face
of the beloved imprinted itself on the lover's heart.
When Astrophel could not write of his Stella,
his muse advised, *Look in thy heart and write!*

But I don't trust my heart these days, too often
a foul cistern breeding toads. So I snap
what is beautiful, this sky and this sea I can love,
and I take them home in a small silver box.

The Jesus Potato

> *. . . the sight of their savior in a potato has
> reinvigorated their faith and their desire to
> help others.*
>
> — FoxNews.com

She wants to believe in miracles—
Mary in a grilled cheese or Jesus in a potato
once intended for a picnic salad.

Her doubting spouse says those weren't miracles.
If Jesus hid in a vegetable, it wouldn't be a potato.
For a second coming, he'd pick something less solid.

She's as likely to find saints or martyrs in marbles,
he adds. She skins, boils, and cubes potatoes,
and silently craves a man less stolid,

one who'd lift spirits, not simply pass the Miracle
Whip and karate-chop potatoes.
She remembers their salad

days, so raw and green it seemed a miracle,
and the Sunday joy of a thick potage,
the dressing on their salad,

and then the undressing, the miracle
of their uncanonized bodies, the piety
of two pairs of lips sealed,

St. Elmo's Fire on the skin, as much a miracle
now as stigmata or Christ on a potato,
altered, anointed, and dumped in a salad.

She envies women the signs in their munchibles,
the St. Petersburg woman who saw Jesus in a potato
chip, crisp wafer preserved like a relic, but salted.

She needs no Michelangelos,
just a split bagel imprinted with a *pietà,*
served with flutes of wine, *Salud! Salud!*

She looks for the Virgin cradling Jesus on pretzels
and chicken breasts with the face of the Pope,
and she prays for vegetables maculate and soiled.

St. Elmo's Fire

Storms bring it in bursts of blue and violet,
atmospheric trick, mystery of light,
illusory corona of fire.
Not fire, but ripped molecules of air.
The phoenix that self-destructs on a pyre,
emerging alive from ashes—merely a myth.
Lightning rods, chimneys, and spires spark and hiss.
Masts of ships conduct it, wings, leaves, and grass.

Other things go up in smoke—hope, dreams, love.
Salamander scampers from a burning log,
flame-chased and scorched—but born from fire?—
illusion, surely, mirage, or sleight of hand—
regenerates its own lost limbs, lucky creature
endures fire and smoke yet suffers no harm.

Flash

Followed by light, a beam on a dark country road.
It happened in one of these, went by the same way.
A kind of dancing, hot and rapid, bodies
swaying and undulating.
An obscene action, it brought out the bad girl in me.
Foreshadower of how, years later, I would be mugged
by waves of heat, cascades of sweat
under my blouse, rivulets into my bra.
What the light was doing. Signal of caution,
a kind of Morse code, an SOS.
Turned on like an idea, a stroke of brilliance,
like a light bulb, on, then off.
The bulb that blinds.
Just how fast it ended.
A flood, it washed over me quickly—
I could have drowned in that melting.
The way lightning sometimes strikes.
Like a streak, sudden and transient.
Abundance of this, but minus cash.
Something in a pan, like fool's gold.
The way he delivered a smile.
Radiant heat.
Something that went back in time, was out of time,
the wrench that fractured time.
Temperature point at which vapors ignite in air.
Cards by which we learn, or don't.
A one letter difference between this and flesh,
that one letter, all the difference.

Ecdysiast

You think it's easy
to unravel the boa of feathers and cast
it off, to turn the act
of undressing into an art, suggest *Yes*
to each hungry face, go just so far and then desist?

Not one can touch, but all must leave feeling sated.

Sequins sparkle as she slinks across the dais,
peels the skirt and tosses it as if rolling dice,
and then the bustier, hook by hook, and thrown aside,
a spider molting, her gaze at once smoldering and icy,
the swivel of hips, to keep the tease slow and steady.

Happy Hour

The chunk of day we appropriate
for happiness, when we will be happy
because that is the appointed hour.
We pour out of offices, factories, and vans.
We gather in gin mills to guzzle
our foamy, pungent, throat-burning
joy. We hoist a few. Some of us crack
jokes. The rest of us toss our heads back,
laugh, and down shots. We order gimlets,
martinis, and cosmopolitans.
We tell work stories. We eat peanuts.
Our happiness is exponentially increased
by the sudden appearance of chicken wings
for which we are almost unspeakably grateful
though each yields no more than a thimbleful
of meat. We toast each other, our health,
better luck next time, and here's to Jackson,
may he rest in peace. Our joy is multiplied
by two while the price of drinks is divided
in half, thus allowing us to drink twice
as much and thereby double our pulchritude.
Someone buys a round for the house.
We drop quarters into the jukebox.
We swing and sway. We stomp on shells.
For sixty full minutes, we are locked
in friendship and love for human creatures.
Our troubles left in the parking lot,
we linger at the bar qualmless, high

on life, some of us so high we levitate.
We raise our glasses: Here's to the gin mills
of America, the taverns, bars, pubs,
road stops, cafés, saloons, and the shot
and beer joints. Here's to the bartenders
and barmaids. Praise to the convivial genius
who invented Happy Hour. Saluté!
Down the hatch! Bottoms up! And cheers!
And if there is weeping, let the tears
be tears of joy. Let the engines idle,
the dark roads remain untraveled.
Let the hands of the clock hold us.

Filbert

It's a runt of a nut,
round and brown as an unsightly molar,
and just as unpopular.
A nut with an identity crisis,
often mistaken for its cousin, the hazelnut.
Cheap substitute for the elegant almond.

No one ever orders filberts by the quarter pound,
as they do peanuts or cashews.
No one pops them into the mouth like candy.
And whoever says, *Once I start eating these filberts,*
there's no stopping me?

It's the same way with people sometimes,
like being unpopular in high school
because you're too fat or have too many pimples,
and everyone picks around you,
fishing for pistachios and exotic Spanish nuts.

You're that kid whose mother named him
Filbert. No way you could ever be cool.
You're that kid whose mother is in and out
of the nuthouse. You go through school excluded
by the versatile pecans, pecked on
by birds and squirrels, subject to blight,
nutty as a jaybird.

Put salt on a magpie's tail, that bird won't fly.
Put salt on a filbert, it soars,

the way the eponymous Carrie did
when she plotted in secrecy how to get even,
then roasted the senior class.

You dream of strutting back like that someday,
the star of your own story,
stripped of your husk and lightly seasoned.
A genuine filbert. Zesty in recipes, mixing it up
at the prom, defiant like a cashew,
green as a pistachio, bold as a Brazil,
hotter than a honey-roasted peanut,
spreading your wings like a shelled walnut.

A Murmuration of Starlings

It was raining dead birds.
—Mayor Brian Levine,
The Star-Ledger, 1/27/09

Starlings dropped from the sky,
mid-flight, like balloons suddenly deflated.

No time to spread their wings and glide on air,
and, synchronized, to soar and dive.

No time to close their wings, to wrap
themselves in shrouds of feathers, and sleep.

They fell like water balloons tossed blindly
from dormitory windows.

They fell like rocks dumped from the unlatched
rear end of a construction truck.

They fell like bombs, like stars, like fallen angels,
they fell like dead starlings.

Hundreds plummeted from the sky
on cars, porches, and snow-covered lawns.

They'd taken the poisoned bait
and, headfirst, dreamed one last time of England.

Birds who'd once disturbed a king's sleep
with cries of *Mortimer, Mortimer.*

Memento mori, forcing us to contemplate
unexpected death.

Do we not already think of the fallen,
earth's fields littered with corpses?

Dark vision made real,
their glistening bodies, silent now and still.

Birds who'd sung their own song
and wooed their mates with lavender and thistle.

Four

Supplication to Water

Afflict me, for I have squandered you on grass
green as money, then cursed you during the draught.

Rinse out my filthy mouth with soap suds.
Abase me and give me a basin.

I have lain down with dogs and consorted with pigs.
Knock me over with fierce waves and splash me.

Load up my bathing suit with rough sand.
Cast me ashore naked and newly abluted.

I have polluted the pristine lake, peed in the pool,
and stolen polliwogs from your pond.

I have scorned the tuna and consumed the babies,
built a city upon you, and prayed for your conversion

to wine. I have failed to hold you throughout the night.
Put a drop in my bucket. Spend me like legal tender.

Catch me between the devil and the deep deep blue.
Let me enter the same river twice, for I am grungy.

Launder me. Liquidate me. Moisten my dry eyes.
Convert my frozen heart to cold hard cash.

Onion

Nine concentric spheres layered around
the heart, perfection of symmetry,
heliocentric, a world embraced.

The heart, a small god at the center,
feels secure, unaware of the knife
on the counter, the bright blade, the hand

that rises. How quickly the circle
is broken, so bloodless a letting
go, how easily the heart slides out.

"Your dreams miss you"

—TV commercial for Rozerem,
a sleep medication

They want you back in bed,
not in the kitchen drinking warm milk,
trying to tire yourself with a Russian
novel or Jay Leno, as you so often do.
Your dreams don't lose faith, don't give up.
They won't abandon you.

Look—snuggled among feather pillows,
the one where you run from something
horrific, the way people flee an inferno,
legs spinning like bicycle wheels,
while the counter-wind holds you in place.

And bundled under the comforter, that loafer
of a dream where you attempt to report
for a new job. You're in the right building,
but can't find the office. You spend
all morning in stairwells and elevators,
racing from room to room, until it's so late
you know they'd never keep someone like you.

Patient and decked out in a silk kimono,
the dream where you're in a fight and you'd beat
your attacker to a pulp if only you could land
a punch. You're ready to cream that punk.
You've got the haymaker, the uppercut

that your son used to call an *apricot.*
You've pummeled the bag—right hook, left jab—
but now when you thrust, you miss him.

Curled up at the foot of the bed,
the dream that's lingered for years.
You're shopping in Sears. Your snow-suited
son acts up, crawls under the clothes racks,
disappears. You haul him into the ladies' room

for a smack on the seat of his pants,
but he's too padded, and he bobs and weaves.
You know if you could just whack him,
he'd never run again. And you wouldn't
duck your dreams, sedate yourself with milk,
and miss all of Jay's punch lines,
wondering where your boy sleeps tonight.

It Runs This Deep

Jesus loves you.
Everyone else thinks you're an asshole.
　　　—bumper sticker

But not your mother.
She remembers the peach she once powdered,
the pink bud unfolding inside,
the symmetry of it, all Renaissance perfection,

a miniature starfish pulsing with life,
small center of her universe, a bull's eye,
little ruby, pinched cherry tomato,
now the target of insults, the butt of jokes.

She remembers how you slid into this world ass first,
a comic reversal forewarning who you would be,
your ID displayed, as if proofed at the door.

She remembers the muffin of your bottom,
split and sprinkled with confectioner's sugar,
the tiny cranberry tucked inside.

No matter how many times she's kicked your ass
out of the house, or how many times you've lost it
at the casinos, or how many times it's been busted
and hauled before the bench,

no matter how many drunk tanks have held you,
your mother remembers when she first held you

and how she loved you, every part of you,
and loves you still,

the lilliputian donut hole,
the dark star puckered like a kiss.

Prunis Persica

Peach whose perfume seduces,
leaves me sticky-fingered,

foraging like a bee into the heart,
where the flesh parts from the pit,

where the promise of peach resides,
my tongue coated with nectar of peach

in this summer lush with peach—
Autumnglo poached from the orchard,

Redhaven naked and eaten whole,
Elegant Lady sun-ripened and slurped—

fragrance of peach on my skin,
peach and poacher meshed,

face flushed with indulgence of peach,
blushed all winter in memory of peach.

You Offer Lychee
to Your American Friends

—for Belle Yang

In the gilded bowl your mother sent from China,
you arrange two pounds of lychee—
strawberry-red, rose-colored, amber-yellow,
all aromatic and heart-shaped,
a bowlful of edible jewels.

You place one in your palm, pinch
the peel, and release the aphrodisiac, lift
the fleshy aril from the seed, roll it
like a luscious grape across your tongue,
then squish.

Your new friends try the lychee,
and spit it out, this favorite fruit of Asian women—
and Yang Yuhuan,
the Emperor's favorite concubine, kept by her bed
such a bowl of desire.

These American women want chocolate—
milk, dark, and bittersweet.
And now you wrinkle your nose.

Belle, your fruit is delicious but chocolate, too,
and because I want to mediate this cultural divide,
I offer you chocolate, hold it out as a soldier does
to a child in the streets of a foreign land.

Here, smell the melted butter, hint of vanilla,
boiling sugar. Learn to love what is decadent,
what grows in other gardens.
Breathe the ghost of cacao tree.
Imagine the thick syrup and the bright red cherry
tucked like a gemstone inside.

Kerfuffle

A nervous shuffle, some kind of fluke,
commotion stirred with his James Dean leer,
the words he spoke, nonsense and fluff,
and yet, he could dishevel and fuel
a firestorm I could feel
throwing me off balance, off my usual keel.
An agitation about the heart, a ruffle
of air. He made me break every rule.
He was onomatopoetic, able to reel
me in, his flurry and fuss a feathered lure—
the stutter and lisp of him, his assonance soft as fur.

Side Effects

He came with a warning label.
He caused headache, dry mouth,
diarrhea, constipation, depression,
severe vomiting, a weak stream,
and a compulsion to gamble.
He was toxic and carcinogenic.
Fish died in the rivers where he swam.
When he opened his mouth,
canaries flew in and expired.
He was every bad habit I ever had.
He was all trans fats and palm oil,
more dangerous than white chocolate.
He was the monosodium glutamate of lovers.
He was the shakes, blurred vision,
restless legs, abdominal bloating,
palpitations, and difficulty swallowing.
He was a four-hour erection.
He was something slipped into a drink,
the Mickey Finn of obsessions.
He was everything in excess,
a massive overdose.
He was my final addiction,
the one I couldn't kick.
He was a lethal injection.

There Where Love Had Been

An echoing chamber now,
the tinny sound of steel,
wind swirling, something gearing up,
the dangerous anticipation
like living in the cone of uncertainty
in those hours before a hurricane hits,
the body not knowing what will be left
standing, knowing already
how a house can crumble,
everything reduced to a pile of rubble,
debris of boards and branches,
tangle of wires,
knowing already the silence,
the ache of emptiness,
the blood-soaked butcher paper
flapping in the street.

The Desolation of Wood

A funnel-shaped cumulonimbus,
violet-blue sky, and three desolate trees,
each with narrow trunk, the barren branches
topped by a strange cluster of leaves,
broad like a mushroom, and vaguely atomic.

The trees stand apart from each other.
They look lonely, as if abandoned,
hungry, as if they want or need something.

I think of Elizabeth who once told me that in China
wood is the fifth element. I want to forget
fire, air, water, and earth, want to believe
the trees are a sign I can be wood.

But wood conspires with dirt,
water uproots trees,
branches sag and snap in unstable air,
crackle and burn in flames.

When the turbulence inside the cloud bursts,
when wind hurls the trees and lightning strikes,
let me be stone, not wood.
Wood houses a past and rots at the heart.

For One Who Crumbles in Spring

Do not rail against the daffodils for their insistence
on yellow, or the iris for being purple and persistent.

Do not curse the bees as they wriggle
their bottoms from honeycombs, nor begrudge them
pollination and flirtation with flowers.

Do not blame the cherry blossoms
for blossoming abundantly and pinkly,
or the grass for growing green, though you have stomped
your foot and beaten it with clenched fists.

Though you long for the desert, parched hills,
burnt weeds, though you will miss the lushness of spring
this year, it will come again.

It will search for you among the beach plums
that year after year emerge from grains of sand
that once were rocks and stones, yet smother themselves
with clusters of white flowers and blue-black fruit.

Five

"How Is a Shell Like Regret?"

—Colette Inez

For years you believe the ocean's inside the shell,
swear you hear the water's swoosh and moan,
as if the shell remembers,
until some scientific killjoy explains
the ear's construction, how enclosure and compression
create an echo chamber within your head.
The sound you hear—pulsation of your blood, he says.
Years later that too is proven wrong. Not water, not blood,
but ambient noise, wavelengths, a mix of frequencies,
exciting the conch's resonant air.

The first shell floats in a salty pool at your feet,
squirmy sea snail long gone, house vacated.
Small fish squiggle in and out.
Every wish you ever wished upon a star,
every miracle you prayed hard for,
every time you went down on your knees and begged God,
every dream that didn't come true,
each huckster, pettifogger, every trickster
and flimflam artist who ever sucked you in.
All illusion of ocean.

Inside that shell, the sound of regret, relentless as any ocean.
It pounds the shore, rises and falls, surges and pulls,
turns over, slides back out again, and keeps on coming.
Heart-shaped, the conch rests in your hand,
hard to fingernail's tap and touch,

shatters if dropped.
Pink at the lip, pearlescent, like skin burned and scarred.

You gather one, another and another, collect them
on windowsills until the house is full.
Sometimes at night you hear a chorus of them singing
through the hard shell of your grief, singing its own song,
so bitter and so sweet.

The Temptation of Mirage

Save your water and green vegetation.
What I want is the desert.

Keep your deciduous pines,
the solace of shade and shadows.

Give me starkness on the horizon,
predictability of beige and brown.

Let me suffer the heat and burn,
air so hot it undulates in sine waves,

and the illusion of water,
the levitation of lake.

Not one human for hundreds of miles,
eternity of sand, an open-air coffin.

Everything fixed and final,
except the night-blooming cereus,

its creamy petals like white silk,
Cinderella in the desert,

narcotic fragrance of the skin,
sweet, juicy pulp of the fruit,

red as a splash of blood,
for one night only, quench of beauty

more real than I can bear,
closed forever by morning sun.

The Very Smell of Him

Body balm, the sharp scent of thistle,
hint of the gym and Irish Spring.
Under his arms, off limits
now, whiff of memory—
late Sundays in bed,
must of his skin,
cinnamon
on toast—
him.

Love Song with Plum

I take what he offers, a plum,
round and plump,
deeper than amethyst purple.
I lift the fruit from his palm.
Like Little Jack Horner, I want it in a pie,
my thumb stuck in to pluck
out that plum.
I want it baked in a pudding,
served post-prandial,
drenched in something potable,
and set on fire, to sit across from him and say, *Pass*
the pudding, please.
Spread on our morning toast, dollops of plum preserves,
and when we grow old, a bowl of prunes,
which, after all, are nothing more than withered plums.
But today the air is scented with plumeria,
and at this particular fruit stand, I'm plumb
loco in love with the plumiest
man. Festooned with peacock plumes
and swaddled in the plumage
of my happiness, I want to stand at the perimeter
of this plum-luscious
earth, sink a plumb
line for balance, then plummet
like a bird on fire, placate
all my desires, my implacable
hunger for the ripeness of my sweetheart's plum.

"No soup for you!"

—The Soup Nazi, *Seinfeld*

Let the people slurp their soup.
They are cold and famished.
They have longings, desires, hungers,
assuageable only by soup.

That girl, appetite voracious but unsated,
bring her to my counter. I will sustain her with soup.
Bring me your hungry, your underfed, your malnourished.
Bring them out of the rain, snow, and sleet.
They have waited in line for hours, wraith-like,
breathing the herb-laced air—saffron, basil, garlic.

Bring me the beggar on the street, the alcoholic,
the dope fiend, the runaway, the hooker, the ex-con.
Bring me your love-starved, sex-starved, soup-starved,
the ones starved for affection, starved for attention,
ravenous for fame, for power, glory, money.
They shall be fed from my stockpot.

Mulligatawny, lentil, mushroom with dill,
beef barley, chicken with pearls of pasta,
hearty split pea with a ham bone.
Soup in bowls, in styrofoam cups, soup in crocks,
in jugs, mugs, and tureens.

That young man at the back of the line,
at the end of his rope, down on his luck,
out of luck, his every hunger unappeased,
he shall have his mother's homemade minestrone.

I believe in the power of soup,
ladled, spooned, and tilted into the hungry mouth.
Soup du jour and soup du nuit.
Gazpacho and bouillabaisse,
onion topped with French bread and melted cheese,
chowder thick with clams, pasta fagioli, and pepper pot.

Bring me the pervert, the hustler, gambler,
crackhead, the tweaker, the man who has lost everything.
Arm them with spoons. Adorn them with bibs.
Let them eat lobster bisque.
Let the earth be loud with the music of their slurping.

Phone in a White Room

A single phone, only thing in a white room.
Mounted on the wall to my right.
Light pours through the windows, pockets
of glare, trellis of shadows, walls of stone.
This is a place of emptiness,
like the place inside me
that waits for the phone to ring,
doesn't want it to ring because it might
be the news I dread—someone I love
not coming home—the hospital or the cops—
that someone sick or in trouble.

The room twists, like Rubik's Cube.
Now the phone's on the floor as if
everyone's moved out or no one's moved in.
An albino of a room.
White as the whale, more terrifying than black.
This is the color of absence.

The room shifts and turns,
a clock that ticks and moves its arms.
The phone's on the opposite wall,
upside down, cord going the wrong direction,
laws of gravity defied.
Light lifts from the floor, crisscross
of shadows like cells in a prison or lunatic asylum.

Someone turns my world upside down.
The phone's on the ceiling, cord dangling

like Tantalus' grapes, and if it rings,
I can't answer. I'm here on the floor, calculating
the shortest distance between two points.
This is the geometry of longing. The circle broken.
It's all perspective, depth, shadows,
and how the light plays out.
It's down to the phone that rings, or doesn't.
So much empty space, all squares and rectangles,
so many straight lines, all hitting hard walls.

Twilight

That time of day when the almost dark slips
through the window and the light diffuses,
no longer daylight, not yet night, that still
blue moment, hesitation between what
was and what will be, blip in Time, dollop
of dough, transitory like pregnancy,
that time of day when she thinks of her child,
the air returning the fragrance of powder,
sweet baby's breath, his lily-soft skin, plump
muffin of his belly, unbroken, unbitten,
unburnt, no knife in sight, delicate as a wafer,
that child more than bread, sustenance
unsustained, his pure buttery goodness
for just that moment filling the room.

Birdhouse

In the garden a single rose,
and though it was a beauty, a brilliant red,
we'd hoped for more, an extravagance of buds,
blossoms, and blooms, visible from our empty house.
We settled for what we could get, then birds
came to the feeder and roused us
with song, music that pierced the heart under the ribs.
Cardinals, goldfinches, nuthatches—some kind of IOU?
a gift of compensation? Not one sour
note sounded from the garden bed.
Profusion of feathers, music, and the persistent scent of rose.

Seventh-Grade Science Project

I ran in a field of wildflowers,
        waving a butterfly net, three
                yards of gauzy fabric stitched

                to the looped rim of a hanger
        stapled to a broom handle.
By summertime my father

had already left with his
        beautiful mistress. Mother
                stayed inside and loafed, said

                she could not watch my tiny
        murders. The field held lemon
lilies, daylilies aflame in orange

and red, buttercups, purple
        clover, and wild roses with
                thorns that cut my arms.

                I caught a black swallowtail,
        monarch, fritillary and mourning
cloak, a painted lady. I learned

how to sneak up on a butterfly,
        its long tubular tongue uncoiled
                inside a flower, and pinch the

folded wings between my thumb
and index finger. I dropped each
hostage onto a wad of Clorox-

soaked cotton inside the kill jar.
I observed the flutter of wings,
the wiggling thorax, and when

the wiggling stopped, I placed
the butterfly on a felt mounting
board. I stuck a straight pin

precisely into the center
of the thorax and eased
the wings apart. Broken

wings or missing antennae
would lose points. I prepared a
data label for each butterfly—name,

date of capture, location—then slid
the bodies inside a shadow box.
The pin-pricked fingers, wasp

stings, and blood on my arms
were what I paid for my first
A in science. All that summer

I ran like something wild and left
my multi-colored fingerprints
on everything I touched.

About the Author

Diane Lockward is the author of three previous poetry collections, most recently, *What Feeds Us,* winner of the 2006 Quentin R. Howard Poetry Prize. Her poems have been selected by Dorianne Laux for the *2008 Best of the Net Anthology* and published in such journals as *Beloit Poetry Journal, Harvard Review, Spoon River Poetry Review*, and *Prairie Schooner.* They have also been featured on *Poetry Daily* and *Verse Daily* and read by Garrison Keillor on NPR's *The Writer's Almanac.* The recipient of a Poetry Fellowship from the New Jersey State Council on the Arts, she has been a featured poet at the Frost Place Conference on Poetry and Teaching, the Burlington Book Festival, and the Geraldine R. Dodge Poetry Festival. She lives in northern New Jersey and can be contacted at her website: www.dianelockward.com

Breinigsville, PA USA
22 March 2011
257992BV00007B/3/P